Holocaust Rescuers

by Gretchen McBride

Editorial Offices: Glenview, Illinois • Parsippany, New Jersey • New York, New York
Sales Offices: Needham, Massachusetts • Duluth, Georgia • Glenview, Illinois
Coppell, Texas • Ontario, California • Mesa, Arizona

Der Führer

XPRIL

16	17	18	19	20		
Sonntag	Montag	Dienstag	Mittwoch	Donnerstag		

Adolf Hitler, shown here in this calendar, ruled Germany from 1933–1945.

Campaign of Hate

Adolf Hitler seized power in Germany in 1933. He died in 1945. From 1933–1945, he carried out a brutal plan to eliminate Europe's Jewish people. Hitler and his Nazi Party claimed that Jews were an "inferior race." He convinced many Germans that the Jews were responsible for Germany's economic problems.

Hitler was able to spread his message of hate by holding huge rallies and giving speeches on the radio. Radio provided an inexpensive way to reach millions of people. Still, there were many people who refused to believe Hitler and the Nazi Party's lies. Some of those people tried to save Jewish people from the certain death that awaited them at Nazi concentration camps.

The Holocaust

Holocaust means "complete destruction by fire." The word is used today to describe the Nazis' plan to wipe out Europe's Jews.

About six million Jews died in the Holocaust. At the same time, a like number of people of many different beliefs and backgrounds were murdered. The Holocaust destroyed lives, families, and whole villages. It came close to ending Jewish life and culture throughout all of Europe.

The Jewish population was *concentrated*, or brought together in one place, at concentration camps such as the one above.

Did people know?

Life became harder for the Jewish people as soon as Hitler took power. Many were taken from their homes and forced into ghettos. These ghettos were areas of cities cut off from the rest of the people. The ghettos were crowded and dirty. The Jewish people were not allowed to leave them. But soon the Nazis came up with a "final solution" to the "Jewish question." They sent the Jewish people to concentration camps to be killed.

People in the United States suspected that something was happening to the Jewish people in Europe. But there was no proof of the Holocaust until 1942. In that year the United States government received a **cable** from **representatives** of the World Jewish Congress in Switzerland. The cable revealed that Hitler was planning to kill millions of Jewish people in Europe.

American President Franklin Roosevelt learned about the Holocaust in 1942.

You might be wondering why the Jews did not leave as soon as Hitler took power. There are several reasons. First, they had no idea of the horror that was to come. The Nazis kept their plans secret. That helped prevent the Jews from fighting back. Most people did not want to leave their homes. It is scary to leave everything behind in order to start a new life somewhere else. The Jewish people did not want to be **refugees.** However, as things got worse, many of them tried to get out of Europe.

Symbols of the Jewish faith such as these were destroyed wherever the Nazis went.

It was not easy for the Jews to leave. Jewish families often had to leave their money behind when they left. The Nazis stamped Jews' passports with the letter "J" so they would be questioned by other countries' officials. Jews also needed a **visa.** A visa is a pass that allows people to enter a country. Many countries would **issue** only a few visas per year.

Did non-Jewish Europeans know what was happening to their Jewish friends and neighbors? Many people did not know how bad the situation was. Others knew that terrible things were happening but did nothing to help. Still, there were a few very brave people who did what they could to help the Jewish people. You will learn about some of those people later in this book.

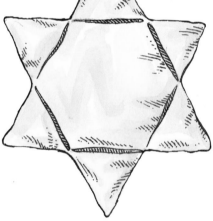

The Nazis forced the Jewish people to wear the Star of David on their clothing so everyone could tell that they were Jews.

Into Hiding

A small number of Jewish people went into hiding in Germany and the other countries that the Nazis took over. Of them, a young girl named Anne Frank, became the most famous. You may have read *The Diary of Anne Frank*. It tells the story of Frank's years spent hiding in the attic of a Dutch office building. The Nazis found Anne and her family. She did not survive.

Anne Frank and her family hid in the attic of the building shown in this cutaway diagram.

There were other Jewish children and adults who were hidden by non-Jewish people. Jews were hidden in attics, cellars, and other places. The people who hid them shared their own food, which during the war was often hard to find.

Some Jewish people tried to "hide in plain sight." This meant they continued to go out in public. However, they hid their Jewish identity. They removed the yellow Star of David that the Nazis made them wear. By doing so they hoped to blend in more. But as "illegals" they could not buy food. This caused many Jewish people to starve to death.

Many of those who hid were captured and killed. Often the people who protected them were also killed. And yet some Jewish people escaped because brave people helped them.

Between the ages of thirteen and fifteen, Anne Frank kept a diary and wrote short stories, essays, and fairy tales. She even began a novel.

Kristallnacht opened the world's eyes to the horror unfolding in Nazi Germany.

Kindertransport: Children's Transport

November 9, 1938, was a turning point for Nazi Germany. On that night the Nazis smashed the windows of Jewish homes and businesses throughout Germany. That night is now known as *Kristallnacht* (KRIS-tahl-nahkt). In English it is often called the "Night of Broken Glass." *Kristallnacht* alerted the world to the danger facing the Jews of Europe. People realized that something had to be done to help the Jewish children trapped in Germany.

After *Kristallnacht*, groups in Britain asked their government to change the laws so that more Jewish children from Germany could enter the country. Ten thousand children managed to get to Britain. Seventy-five hundred of them were Jewish.

The *Kindertransport* saved many Jewish children from certain death.

Children who were homeless, orphaned, or had parents in concentration camps were the first to get visas. But only children who had found people to pay their living costs in Britain were issued visas. The rescue effort was called *Kindertransport*. The word meant "children's transport."

The children traveled by train and then by ship to Britain. Upon arriving in Britain some went to live with foster families. Others were housed in hotels and on farms. The rescuers who organized the *Kindertransport* hoped that the children would rejoin their parents after the war. But when the war ended an awful truth was revealed. Almost all of their parents had died in concentration camps. After the war the children became citizens of Great Britain, Israel, the United States, Canada, and Australia.

Emergency Rescue Committee: Varian Fry

In 1940 a group of New Yorkers formed the Emergency Rescue Committee (ERC). The ERC was concerned about the safety of Jewish writers, artists, and educators. Many of them had fled to France before the war. But then the Nazis conquered most of France in May 1940. The Nazis' control of France placed these Jews in danger. The ERC responded by deciding to try a secret rescue mission.

The journalist Varian Fry was sent by the ERC to Marseille (mahr-SAY). Marseille was located in a part of France that was not directly ruled by the Germans. Fry opened an office in Marseille. He pretended that he was running a charity. In reality Fry used the office to help Jewish people escape to safety. The French government soon became suspicious of Fry. They made him leave France in 1941. But in just thirteen months, Varian Fry had helped more than two thousand people leave Nazi-occupied France. Among them were some of the most famous artists and thinkers of the twentieth century.

"All of his hearers were greatly interested and impressed by what he said. . . . It is evident that Mr. Fry is exceptionally well informed regarding the France of today and the most prominent Frenchmen. Mr. Fry has a good voice and a pleasant delivery."

—ROBERT ERSKINE ELY,
Executive Director,
The Economic Club of New York

"Immediately after his return from France, Mr. Fry spoke at several Foreign Policy Association meetings. He was uniformly enthusiastically received by the audience. His sincerity and effective platform manner combine to make him an excellent speaker."

—FRANCES J. PRATT, *Director,*
Speakers Bureau, Foreign
Policy Association

© Fabian Bachrach

VARIAN FRY

Fifteen Months in France and Portugal
European Director, Emergency Rescue Committee

—LECTURES—

FRANCE UNDER PETAIN

AFTER THE WAR, WHAT?

AMERICA'S FOREIGN POLICY TOWARD FRANCE

WANTED BY THE GESTAPO
Rescuing Refugees in France, Spain and Portugal

Varian Fry (above) saved almost two thousand Jews during World War II by setting up a pretend charity fund in Marseille, France (left).

Le Chambon-sur-Lignon

The French village of Le Chambon-sur-Lignon (ler shahm-BOHN ser lin-YOHN) gave shelter to Jews during the war. The people of the village were mainly Protestant Christians. This made them a minority in France, where most people were Catholic Christians. As minorities the Protestants sympathized with the Jews and wanted to help them.

Andre Trocme, a church pastor, urged the people to give aid to their Jewish neighbors. The people

Le Chambon-sur-Li

responded by allowing Jews to hide in their homes. Other Jews were given shelter by Catholic Christians in Catholic buildings near the village. The villagers also helped some Jews obtain fake visas to enter Switzerland. Switzerland was not involved in the war. That made it safer for Jews to live there.

The people of Le Chambon-sur-Lignon did not feel that they were doing anything heroic. They simply made an **agreement** with Pastor Trocme to do the right thing. In doing so, they helped almost five thousand Jewish people survive the Holocaust.

o Loire) – Alt. 9f0ᵐ – Cure d'Air
Roches

A postcard from 1942 (left) showing a children's home in Le Chambon-sur-Lignon.

Refugee children with their guardian (below) outside of a children's home in Le Chambon-sur-Lignon.

Raoul Wallenberg, Heroic Diplomat

More than anyone else, Raoul Wallenberg is remembered for having saved Jewish people from the Holocaust. Wallenberg was born in Sweden in 1912. He came from a wealthy family. In 1935 he graduated from the University of Michigan with a degree in architecture. Wallenberg had difficulty finding architectural work in Sweden. So he went to work in Palestine (now Israel). There he met Jews who had escaped from Nazi Germany.

In 1944 the United States established the War Refugee Board (WRB) to help save Jewish people. The WRB's representative in Sweden brought together a group of people who wanted to organize a rescue mission in Budapest, Hungary. The group asked Wallenberg to lead the rescue mission. He accepted and became a **diplomat.**

Raoul Wallenberg

At the time, the Nazis were losing control of Hungary to the Russian army. The Russians were taking over very quickly. So the Nazis worked as fast as they could to deport Hungary's Jews to concentration camps. Raoul Wallenberg felt there was no time to follow the usual rules of diplomacy. He used any means he could to save Jewish people.

The people who worked under Wallenberg issued thousands of protective passes. Wallenberg also had "Swedish houses" built in the city. He used his position to declare the houses Swedish territory. Jews were safe at the "Swedish houses" because Sweden, like Switzerland, was neutral. That meant it wasn't involved in the war. Soon diplomats from other neutral countries followed Wallenberg's example.

Jewish people going to one of Wallenberg's "Swedish houses" in Budapest

The Nazis would fill train cars with Jewish people to take them away to concentration camps. Wallenberg climbed onto the tops of the train cars and passed protective passes to the people inside them. He then would jump to the ground and demand that the people with passes be released. The guards had orders from their **superiors** to shoot Wallenberg. But they were so impressed by his amazing courage that they allowed him to escape unharmed.

In January 1945 the Nazis planned to kill the last remaining Jews of Budapest's largest Jewish ghetto. At this point, it was clear that Germany would be defeated. Raoul Wallenberg threatened the general who had been ordered to carry out the killings. Wallenberg said that if the order were carried out, he would have the general executed as a war criminal following Germany's defeat. Thanks to Wallenberg's brave threats, the people of the ghetto were saved at the last minute.

When the Soviet troops marched into Hungary, Wallenberg asked permission to visit their military headquarters. He was never seen again. Wallenberg's fate is unknown. Nevertheless this courageous man was able to save as many as 100,000 Jewish people from the Nazi concentration camps.

The Nazis transported people to concentration camps on freight trains such as this one, shown after the war ended.

The Danes

The Nazis occupied Denmark during most of World War II. Despite the occupation, many Danes refused to help the Nazis murder the Jews. A courageous German diplomat, Georg Ferdinand Duckwitz, secretly told the Danes that the Nazis were about to deport all of the Jewish citizens of Denmark. The Danes acted quickly. They hid some Jewish people. They helped others leave the country. For two weeks, Danish fishermen ferried Jewish people across the water to Sweden. This was a nationwide effort. More than seven thousand Jewish Danes were saved.

Georg Ferdinand Duckwitz

This Danish fishing boat was used to rescue Jewish refugees. It is on display at the Holocaust Memorial Museum in Washington, D.C.

A Jewish family from Denmark
shares Christmas dinner with
a Christian family in Sweden.
The Danes saved approximately
seven thousand Jewish people
during World War II.

Remembering: Yad Vashem

The Hebrew phrase *yad vashem* can be translated as "a monument and a memorial." The Israeli government founded Yad Vashem to help preserve the memory of Holocaust victims. The organization is in charge of many museums, libraries, memorials, and monuments. Yad Vashem's Avenue and Garden of the Righteous Among the Nations, in Jerusalem, Israel, honors the non-Jewish people who risked their own lives to save Jews during the Holocaust.

The Hall of Remembrance (below) is found in the Holocaust Memorial Museum in Washington, D.C.

This Holocaust memorial sculpture (below) is located in Berlin, Germany.

Glossary

agreement *n.* an understanding between people, groups, or nations.

cable *n.* a message sent through wires by electric current or electronic signals.

diplomat *n.* someone who manages the relations between his or her nation and other nations.

issue *v.* to send out; put forth.

refugees *n.* people who flee for refuge or safety.

representatives *n.* people appointed or elected to speak for others.

superiors *n.* people of higher position, rank, or ability.

visa *n.* an official signature or endorsement upon a passport.